NIXES MATE REVIEW

ISSUE 34|35 WINTER|SPRING 2025

Nixes Mate Books
Allston, Massachusetts

Book design by Michael McInnis
Cover image from the collection of Lauren Leja
Colorized by Michael McInnis

Philip Borenstein · Publisher Emeritus
Hannah Larrabee · Editor + Explorer
Michael McInnis · Designer + Factotum
Annie Elezabeth Pluto · Editor + Director

ISBN 978-1-949279-61-0

Nixes Mate Publications
POBox 1179
Allston, MA 02134
nixesmate.pub

Kidnapped off the streets, migrants and citizens remain ghosts in an unrecognizable America. Where once the ocean nourished and protected us, it now becomes a great moat. Our ports drain away the tides of ships. We are asked to endure and sacrifice. We are all shipwrecked after a three hour cruise. *Alas, Poor Gilligan! I knew him, Horatio: a fellow of infinite jest, of most excellent fancy...*

Nixes Mate headquarters at high tide.

Contents

Table of

Alex Carrigan

Theseus accepted the yarn without thinking of what she sacrificed for it. How she gathered her fallen strands of hair since she was a child and weaved them continuously. Her fingers calloused as she spent her youth on this task. She was hopeful her labor would end the violence. When she offered the yarn to Theseus, she didn't tell him what it was made of. She did hope that he'd notice if he stopped for rest in the labyrinth. But he left the string behind when he came out with the minotaur's head. That should have warned her that he'd eventually leave her behind too.

Negative Capability in Ordinary Life

David P. Miller

A man stands
arm's-length
from a wall full
of bookcases.

Hands
clasped in back
of his back:
one grasps
the other.
His trunk
shields both
from books.

His sight
shifts sideways,
up and down,
across lettering.

His head
pivots. One
crabwise step.

An abrupt arm
unfolds
toward a shelf.
Fingertips
atop a book.

The paper block
speaks to his
finger ridges.
He does not move.

Reader, let's pause,
with Keats,
in uncertainties, mysteries,
doubts, without
any irritable reaching
after fact and reason.

Arm extended,
resting hand.

Alex Stolis

I dreamed of faith, hope. I dreamed you again.
The air, winter cold but no snow, no ice.
In the middle of a raging river, I was serene.
You, on shore, skirt aflutter in a wind I didn't feel,

the air, winter cold but no snow, no ice.
I've always been afraid of water. Never learned to swim,
you, on shore, skirt aflutter in a wind I didn't feel;
felt the ocean, tasted salt in the air.

I've always been afraid of water. Never learned to swim;
the river turned to black sheets of rain, I felt your lips,
felt the ocean, tasted salt in the air.
The moon was a sun, there were no stars.

The river turned to black sheets of rain, I felt your lips
your not quite smile when you tease me.
The moon was a sun, there were no stars.
I woke, heard my heart beat, caught a scent of you,

your not quite smile, when you tease me.
Your leg wrapped 'round mine, fingertips tendering my neck,
I woke, heard my heart beat, caught a scent of you.
Of course you weren't there. Yes. You were.

Widow Remembering the Camargue, Its Horses: A Constance of Shifting

Mary Pinard

Coats of salt, manes like white linen, and the wind, the horses there
are the living anchors of the delta, drained by the Rhône, which by
the time it reaches this particular shore of the Mediterranean, has
already traveled at least 500 miles – more if you count the braiding
and unbraiding along and through it branchings. Everything's in a
constant state of revision, including the *etangs*, salt water lagoons,
remnants of old arms and legs of the body of the river, emerging
and disappearing, ghostlike. Even when we were there that summer,
so long ago, it felt illusory, the many-stranded alluvium piling and
unpiling its sediment – the hard remorse of sand carried in its muds
and made from everything before. And that slanting, gold light.

> Together there, our
> long apartness already
> gauzy in my heart.

Remembering Stones

Susan Michele Coronel

Ten hands can't bring back the dead, any more than a tapered candle
or starched collars and cuffs. A wooden table contains stains that
spread like maps, dividing dead from alive & here from *back then*.
When I was ten, my cousin David had a seance in the basement of
his Pittsburgh home. His sister Michelle turned off all the lights.
The anticipation was intoxicating creaks & coins in darkness. At the
same time in a town in Poland, a group of stolid male cousins was
doing the same thing in the back room of a tavern. It snowed the first
snow that evening: shattering puffs of white, snowdrifts the height
of fledgling apple trees. The bark was partly covered, & on the stove,
plates of red meat & whisky. In the distance a neighbor's mangy dog
howled. No one ever returned here, no one emerged from beyond.
But the air was full of living memory, more than headstones could
ever record, or the final dust of cremation. Loved ones' footsteps
could not vanish – not their voices, not their fingers brushing your
hair at night. The glare of streetlights stained the windowpanes as
frost emerged like smoke.

I am split in twain
singing about the damage
remembering stones

William Ross

On studying Picasso's "Guernica,"
> *the evening news in the background*

watch the horse eat that light bulb while
> Scientists predict a rise in sea level of two feet
the lady with the dead baby is going to bite down
> Within the next ten years,
on the mouth of that wall-eyed bull
> The entire eastern seaboard under water, and
a man on fire his hands to the sky
> The summers so hot the only water sea water.
and people dying in the war against the earth

On the Fourth Day

Gloria Mindock

UKRAINE: Oxana witnesses a man being raped by a soldier

SERBIA-HERZEGOVINA: 20,000 women screamed

IRAN: Malakah wore no head scarf when she sang

GEORGIA: Kateran said this president is not my president

RUSSIA: Passports taken so life will get rough for the Uzbeks

SYRIA: Dreams die for young girls

GEORGIA: Images of those beaten are hung on Christmas trees

LEBANON: Hezbollah will kidnap you

RUSSIA: Visit the mafia in Moscow

IRAN: 901 dissidents spoke out

USA: Biden is no longer president

USA: Now what?!

THE WORLD: Blind but waking up

"They" are coming for you with a weapon
in apartment buildings and on the street
Degrading you, stripping you of any justice

"They" are coming for you with a weapon
confiscating your body until dead

Brad Rose

I was just phoning it in – you know, like I was on automatic – when I realized, Maybe I'm on the wrong planet? Of course, happiness depends on your longitude as well as your latitude, but isn't that always the way? Ever since I finished my treatment, I've been rehearsing my mind-reading skills and listening to the fumes as often as I can. After all, why lower your standards? In fact, whenever I carry my cross bow, I don't like to mess around. Not since the incident in the checkout line at that big box store. At least, I gave everybody a warning. Well, almost everybody.

I Killed a Rattlesnake in Texas

Roseanne English

I was running on a back-trail and came across
a woman and her dog. She was yelling *back, back*
and throwing flat, gray stones at the snake's head,
hoping to kill it – it blocked our path. I wanted
to be involved. I don't know why. Animal
instinct, saving the dog, telling a good
story. So I took a big rock and hurled it –
I flattened its head. Its bottom jaw jutted out,
its teeth went crooked. Then I went home
to New York and told everyone at work about it.
I said, *I delivered the killing blow*. I read
rattlesnakes grow by the bushel there in Texas.
There's so many, they have round-ups
to kill them and eat them, in Sweetwater.

Forty-seven

Jennifer Markell

We look at each other like unknowable
planets. Decades later
a newly elected president would be king.
I watch people walk down the street
and wonder what unseen star we're circling.

After an Executive Sells All his Shares (poem found in the news)

L. Acadia

Under Xi,
nobody wants to be
the
richest man in China.

Sarah Carleton

By the time we knew what was happening
we couldn't work out how to watch it without
burning our eyes, so we baked bread instead, noting

the light out the patio door: bright and gloomy,
as if a thunderhead were hovering
over the roof just beyond our line of sight.

I blamed a lack of boxes to poke apertures into,
and when other solutions appeared on Facebook
– colanders, holey objects–

I thought of how years ago, my husband woke
at two a.m. and put on hat and snow boots
to view the aurora borealis

while I stayed in bed, unable to leave my warm sleep.
Now the sun is direct and dazzling, the air
open-window dry, the celestial do-si-do having

scrubbed the humidity from our collective
lens, as if the sky saved an extra miracle
for us in case we missed the first one.

Penelope's Dreams

Ann Hostetler

There's no cell service on Ithaca.
Only stone ruins and fragrant wild thyme.
The boat comes once a week with mail
and supplies – fresh fruits and vegetables,
fine woolens for her tapestries. The roosters
eat scraps from her table. She sends
for chicks who will become hens, lay eggs.
Along with unweaving her day's work,
at night she writes poems in her dreams.
Something to live for during
all that waiting. And if she learned
to love her solitude, what then?
It's the 21st century, but he still holds
the purse strings. When he returns
she is kind to him. Helps him arrange
doctors' appointments for his ailing heart,
reminds him to drink water. On this island
he can't read on screens before bedtime.
His sleep improves. "It's so comfortable here."
And yet, next week the boat
will carry him away again, to his work
and Calypso, the terrible obstacles he says
he conquers so she can live in peace.

Jonathan Blunk

A figurehead mounts the foaming sea at dusk when waves become dark green
and turn to black. The tines of a fork score the water to row the sinking ship to port.

We stand at the ship's rail to share a cigarette, the common brand: *le Gris* – our words
and smoke torn apart by the wind.

Here's to the real world at rest. To scudding white and the light's reflections.
To woodgrain solid as a table, the table consuming a glass, to a box of matches,
each angle affixed.

Some untold gladness must lie hidden here, within reach.

Belfast Maine

Kevin McLellan

The crab apples
        falling. Father

        there. Mother
too. The apples
        kept falling

        onto the car
overlooking the Atlantic.
Father and mother

outside
        the car. Salt
        air. Apples

        bobbing in
the Atlantic
air. More

thuds. The car
a soundtrack. More
salt. No talking

the day the crab apples
        fell in Belfast.

Lauren Leja

We are haunted by the ghosts of America.

The unspooling of history melts into our memories, hovers over our dreams, half remembered, mis-remembered. Cloudy worlds expand, accidental twins multiply, this shadow time is created for us and covers us in the warm blanket of nostalgia.

In each of these photographs dueling dualities form from the spontaneous mechanical defect of the double exposure.

35B45

CREAM
AND SODA

Kurt Schmidt

WHEN SOMEONE ASKED ME if I had a connection to any notable ancestors, I said the Gallup family was one of the oldest to cross an ocean and settle in America. My mother, Elizabeth ("Betty") Gallup, was born in Medford, Massachusetts, in 1915. The patriarch of my mother's family, Captain John Gallop, was born 324 years earlier in 1591 in Mosterne, County Dorset, England.

Captain Gallop sailed for Boston on March 20, 1630 on the *Mary and John*. Once settled, he acquired a vessel, engaged in coastal trade, and became a pilot for ships entering Boston Harbor. Gallop's wife, Christobel, did not travel to Boston with him, staying behind with their four children. John Gallop became important to the development of trade between the Massachusetts Colony and Connecticut and Rhode Island. Governor Winthrop was eager to keep him in America and not see him return to England to be with his family. So Winthrop wrote to Reverend John White in England and asked him to persuade Christobel to come to America. She and her children arrived on September 4, 1633, following a rough 8-week voyage on the *Griffin*.

On that ship were also two historic characters: Reverend John Cotton and Elder Thomas Leverett. John Gallop piloted *Griffin* through the harbor via a new channel that he had discovered. Gallop was said to have been better acquainted with the harbor than any other man of his time. Gallop's Island in Boston Harbor still bears his name.

He gained fame when, in 1636, after a desperate encounter off Block Island, he recovered a vessel that had been captured by the Narragansett Indians from his friend, John Oldham, whom they had killed. This is supposed to have been the first engagement ever between the inhabitants of the American colonies and enemies afloat. The next year, 1637, he took part in the Pequot War with

Massachusetts forces. He also participated in King Philip's War and was a renowned Indian interpreter.

My mother's father, Oren Oliver Gallup, was an expert in trade too, albeit three centuries after his famous ancestor. In the 1900's, Oren wrote articles for export trade journals and for the *New York Times*. Early in his career, he was exporter for Simond Saw and Steel Company of Fitchburg, Massachusetts, and later formed his own export company in New York City. He went to Washington during World War II to head up the export division of international price control.

When I was about eleven, my mother put me on a plane so I could spend my spring school vacation with her parents at their apartment in New York City. Sometime during my vacation week, Grandpa and I took the subway to Yankee Stadium. Grandpa parted his white hair in the middle with precision but often had smudges on his wire-rimmed eyeglasses. I liked his soft voice, easy grin, and the smell of his cigars. Grandpa said he'd been to almost every country in the world, even Russia. There was something about the swaying and squealing of the train, something about all the strange-looking passengers, something about the city smells that made the subway seem magic. Inside the stadium, Grandpa bought a round Yankee patch made of felt that Grandma sewed onto my jacket later. Other days Grandpa took me to the Hayden Planetarium and to his office, where he gave me foreign stamps for my collection.

Years later, when he was elderly, Grandpa flew with Mom to my graduation ceremony at Michigan State University. He had tears in his eyes then, perhaps because he and Grandma had two daughters but no sons. Shortly before he died, he gave me his IBM Selectric typewriter, on which I proceeded to write my first published novel, *Annapolis Misfit*. I thought my grandfather had brought me good luck. Not until my cousin researched our ancestry did I know Grandpa had done more than open up my world. He was my connection to history.

As a young, single woman, Grace Gardner traveled from her home in Medford, Massachusetts around 1910 to teach school in Troy, New Hampshire. She met Oren Gallup in the social milieu of Fitzwilliam's Laurel Lake, where he'd come to build a cottage with a friend. Oren and Grace married and bought a slate-roof summer house next to the Whipple farm and near the lake. She did not want a lakeside cottage where any toddlers were bound to fall in the water and drown. As a woman who spoke softly, it was her determined way of making decisions without fear that they might be controversial.

In 1919, during one of Oren's long business trips in Europe as an export manager, Grace decided to board a Finnish ship leaving New York so that she and their four-year-old daughter could meet Oren in Paris and travel back with him after a tour of Europe. Photographs show Grace and my future mother bundled against the November cold on the hurricane deck of the S.S. *Lapland* – Grace in a stylish long black coat, wide-brim hat, and black leather boots; Betty in heavy wool from head to foot. On the return voyage, Grace was sick the entire trip, not from the sea, but from a pregnancy that would result in a miscarriage. The birth of my Aunt Louise came a couple years later.

My future mother, Betty, grew into a honey-haired beauty. At twenty-one, after quitting Wheaton College and taking a sales job at Macy's, she was spending free time at a neighborhood home where young adults came together for card games and a beer. It was there that Isolde introduced Betty to her handsome brother, Rolf, and soon the two were spending time nearby at his family's home. Two pregnancies occurred there, and each time Rolf said he was not in a position to marry while still living at home and taking night classes at Rutgers. So Betty's father took her for abortions in Brooklyn. After abortion #2, Grace phoned Rolf's mother, who seemed oblivious to the couples' upstairs shenanigans while listening to Sunday radio concerts of New York Philharmonic in his bedroom. The two mothers agreed a marriage should occur before Child #3, which turned out to be me about a year after their marriage.

On my third birthday, Mom was in the Presbyterian Hospital in Newark, New Jersey, giving birth to my sister, Donna. My father was sneaking a woman into our Newark apartment (according to a friend who told Mom later). I was in my grandparent's New York City apartment. Grandma Grace photographed me staring at a long single candle (she must not have had three) atop a chocolate cake. The next day she guided me to a barbershop for a first haircut that sheared off the blonde curls that Mom so cherished. (Grandma would later tell Mom, "You have your girl now. It was time for Kurt to look like a boy.")

Grandma parted her black hair in the middle of her scalp and tied it into a bun in back. She wore simple dresses, square-heeled shoes, and a tight smile to hide her crooked teeth. In New Hampshire during the summer, she fashioned a pole rod to help me catch fish off the Holmes sisters' dock. I spent quiet time with her, learning a card game called Canasta. I cried the first time that she won, not realizing she had allowed me to win for what she considered a reasonable amount of time.

When I was seven, my family left our city apartment and moved to my grandparents' summer house. We spent our first winter there adjusting to a wood stove and hand pump in the kitchen and an outhouse at the rear of the shed. And the cold. But Mom wanted to raise her children in the tranquility of this beautiful region, where she and her sister had spent so many childhood summers. Grandma continued to spend summers with us; Grandpa commuted occasionally by train from New York.

During my school spring vacation trips to New York City, the first thing Grandma and I usually did together upon my arrival was to have a Canasta battle. On other days she took me to the Central Park Zoo and to Radio City Music Hall, where once we saw dancing girls called Rockettes and a romance movie. A Canadian Mountie was kissing some woman hard on the lips and singing to her. Grandma was wiping her eyes with a tiny white handkerchief. We also took long walks along Riverside Drive. As her first grandchild, I seemed to bring her a joy that I never understood at the time.

Although I lived in other places when I was younger, my wife and I have now lived in Grandpa's and Grandma's old summer house for thirty-five years, made some renovations, and raised a child here. Shelley has planted many flowers around the house, and we still have a huge pink bush that was small when my grandmother planted it. The tiny blue spruce given by a friend when our son was born is now fifty feet high. Shelley and I often take a midday walk along the shore of the lake where my grandfather canoed with my future mother so that his little girl could pick water lilies.

Often as I pass through a room, I feel my grandparent's presence and love. I remember their quiet way of teaching me about life and how they loved to introduce me to the wonders of this world.

Standing before my grandparent's headstones at the town cemetery, I remember Grandma's concern for my three-year-old appearance and the lost curls. I'd cultivated the curls again in my thirties but have lost them now in old age. I also remember that Captain John Gallup, and later his wife and children, crossed a tempestuous ocean to settle in America and which eventually led to my having the good fortune of growing up in the land of opportunity.

William Webb

Once the porpoise is out of water
I know it is time to go,
the story of swimming miles in the bay
is past tense
feels like showing off
without my goggles nearby.

I cried when she said from the stage
Those of you who have dogs understand
and I did and I wanted licks and love
cried too when the fellow said
he was sick, but for
different reasons. Los Angeles
a pick-up truck, now a bike, those ears.

Riverside drive and leaves and mums
some kids and a clean bathroom
the old lady in a long black coat
we think ran away from her attendant
that story too because I wanted it for me
to be found,
and steered gently home.

It Might Not Be Cancer

Kerry Trautman

When you say
olive-sized
is it black or green?

This breast
would hardly fill
a martini glass.

Cans come small,
medium, jumbo
or sliced.

Might not.
I am
not mighty.

Kalamata maybe?
Brined with
a stony pit?

For now I can only
raise a toast to
might not.

Shaken,
with a twist,
ice cold.

Christy Prahl

I will never not love a drunk is the truth.
My grandfather tends his potatoes in the field
while my sister and I sell cut flowers
in front of a withering barn.
Who can resist two small girls
handling money?
Aren't we adorable?
Don't our flowers look pretty
and smell like rich people's soap?

These are the days before two girls
alone on the road will prompt
a call to Child Services.
Our grandfather is right there
in the field, we say,
picking dinner.
His breath smells of grandfather
because we don't yet know
the smell of gas-station brandy.

His stories are funny,
the way he hiccups over them
and lets us finish his sentences
when he's lost in the buttons of his shirt.

He loves the ponies and so do we,
but we mean different things by ponies.

Later I come to love that aftershave
of slur that takes me back
to phosphorous in dirt.

(My compass always points east
to vermiculite).

I love that familiar perfume
on the life of the party.
I love the hard way bubbling men
hold my body *(like religion*
is how it feels) and the hard secrets
they tell me after everyone has left.

I love them as a wound
that needs five stitches.
I carry a needle and thread.

When fists punch a wall
avoiding my shoulder
I beg them to stop,
maybe just a week
to see where it goes.

I stick around one more day
and then another in case
they learn to be gentle with me.

They won't quit for good
till I'm altitudes gone
and then turn immaculate
with children and jobs
and telephones they answer.

That smell of hops coming
off the next confession?

It's the stamp of
my never enough.

Kyle Potvin

"Rolling me over the waves will shoulder me under."
—Virginia Woolf, *The Waves*

Despair is a tricky thing. I
inch toward the promise of waves and brave in,
shaded by a pod of pelicans, a masterful V
above me. I
pray for something. Something is dissolving. My toes
press away sand, unsteadying me. I
exhale into water the temperature of air, absorb
algae light, kelp hair aswirl.
Right now, what's wrong with ease?

It's 6 a.m. and a woman walks into the sea

Kyle Potvin

"We may sink and settle on the waves."
—Virginia Woolf, *The Waves*

I have watched this sea for 85 days.
For the first time, pelicans perch on morning tides

as if finding sustenance – or fascination –
in the movements of this woman.

Does she, too, feel everything has changed?
No more briny sea scent. Scant shells to save.

From the balcony, I can almost feel the disappearing
sand spiraling away beneath her bare feet.

Collapse of steadiness with each crash
against her shins.

One more wave and her misty figure could buckle
at the knees, skirt a billowing parachute.

I want her to feel nothing,
water the temperature of air.

Jennifer Franklin

"With the sound of the sea in their ears, vines, meadows rivulets about them, they
are even more aware than we are of a ruthless fate. There is a sadness at the back of
life which they do not attempt to mitigate."
—Virginia Woolf, *On Not Knowing Greek*

I know you were here twice – twenty-six years apart, same
as the span between my two visits. I see you walk past
the shaggy goats just before you felt *the joy of smelling*
a dead horse in a field. Like the ancients, you understood
deep grief is indescribable– Cassandra seeing plundered Troy
and uttering *the naked cry* – the same sound I made
when the pediatric neurologist gave me my daughter's diagnosis.
The sound you uttered when you knew the last letter
you would ever write was your suicide note. *Alive*
to every tremor and gleam of existence, when you choose
the stones to line your pockets a week after you tried but failed
to drown, did you have the sound of the Ionian Sea in your ears?
Did you think of Sappho soaring off a cliff? Did you think of Delphi
when you ate grapes right off the vine, warmed through by the sun.

Fata Morgana

Annie Bolger

it's happening again. this time,
we are on one of those godforsaken beaches
you always took me to on our anniversary, a bracing
new england october beach, where the sand
is ash grey, and the water is yawning black, and
the place where they meet is violent – but this time
it is nearly night, and the boundaries between sky,
sea, and sand are blurred, and this time I am
scared of the waves sneaking up & dragging us under
before vomiting us back up onto the shore to lie
waterlogged, limp, and kelp-like,

and when I turn to tell you I am scared I see you
smiling, fiercely, with all your teeth, and the wind
yowls back at both of us, filling my gums
with the taste of salt, and I am still scared, and alive,
and the wind is alive, and the water is alive,
and the dead kelp is alive,
and the invisible fish churning in the water

with their tiny ancient brains
are so, so alive.

Lisa Schapiro Flynn

I'm twelve hours post-op, and the nurses' voices
say the bodies were found – the dead president's son,
his wife and her sister.

Two days and a naval funeral – gunmetal water fills
the screen of the wall-mounted TV. I can control it
with a button on a box hooked to the bed –

but every channel is the same. An American flag,
whipping, voiced over. The word tragic
until midnight. Nothing else but sleep

until 2 AM, when the next bed begins keening,
calls again and again to her dead husband
begs him to cut the clot boots off her legs.

If I'm sleeping, swimmers are yelling underwater,
padding hands through cracked fuselage, rooting bodies
from cold swells. One of them is mine, I'm sure,

in the green shadow of the Vineyard,
a hundred other wrecks. It's me, it's my dissolving cast
of plaster, the tendrils melting into sea, nimbus

illuminating my beautiful corpse. If I'm awake,
I'm plumbing the nurse button, my sewn neck locked
on a dead, wet pillow, and I can't

fit any more members of that family
into this bed.

Tidal Forces

Ann E. Wallace

Hurricane Gloria lashed and churned
over my New England hometown

on my father's birthday when I was fifteen,
and I walked onto the stone jetty at the beach

with my brother. I can feel the push
and pull of gale forces against my thin

body still, water spraying from ocean
and sky at once, my flapping clothes damp

and heavy, coated in a mist of wet sand.
I trusted my brother. But we should not

have been standing on that rocky pier,
as waves crashed at our feet and the hurricane

roiled around us, flooded streets and splintered
boats. Now, I question his judgment, imagine

how fast we might be swept into the swell.
My mother would have been distressed

had she known he took me into the heart
of the storm. But we made it home that day,

with blurry photos to mark our victory.
It was another forty years before a storm

barreled through my brother's body,
sent him tumbling to his death.

I stand here in the wake, reeling
from the force of it all.

Text Messages from J. (found poem)

L. Acadia

Look what I found while I ransacked the closet!
Actually several weeks ago.
I usually put it in my pocket and rediscover it over and over for years.
In your case, you've been in my suitcase.
I have lots of dead people in my pockets,
a Canon,
and some newlyweds.

Melanie DuBose

Today I walked past the house of longing, past the just ok restaurant of regret on my way home. People touched their fingers to their heads while thinking. Everyone was drinking something. Everything is always present. All my old friends and even my mother call my name. This is not a dream. This is the house of memory. Here I hang pasta on dishtowels on the back of chairs to dry, cook sauces for hours, flowers open quickly like hands spread in surprise. My mother waves a wooden spoon. We tell stories that change with every telling, of a madras skirt, a fortune teller. We lose our shoes in the surf of a sudden wave. My sailboat capsizes. There is a new arrival who reminds us of the hot dog sliding down your body leaving a yellow slash outside the British Museum. My younger self comes and sits beside me, and I am so glad she is not ashamed to see what I have become.

The Excellence Award

Alice Waldert

In first grade, my teacher had us
draw a swan on a river, she held

mine up to show the class – pointed
to my swan's long S-shaped neck,

declared – *This is beautiful!*
On the last day of classes, three grades

sat in the gymnasium. A crowd of parents
stood at the back. The Principal

on microphone demanded quiet.
My teacher appeared on the podium

she called me with six others to the stage
and bestowed on each of us our awards–

ten bold letters stitched on a sliver of fabric,
I squeezed it in my hand. Parents sprang

forward, I searched their faces for my foster
mother's, she wasn't there. My teacher said –

I invited your mother! I looked then for my
biological mother, she too wasn't there.

My foster sister waved to me. When we
arrived home, she showed my award

to her mother – *Look what Alice won!*
She studied the embroidered letters

and asked her daughter –
Why didn't you win this?

Richard Hoffman

save on sleep number beds you won't believe
how they look today erase those wrinkles fast
this simple trick is guaranteed to relieve
new shocking revelations from the past
forget viagra try this simple trick tonight
exclusive brain enhancer get yours free today
12 travel destinations book your flight
new snoring fix a genius hack brief survey
completely empty your bowels stop joint pain
fungus free nails for summer subscribe now
one dose daily is the key rewire your brain
click here defeat anxiety let us show you how
are you over 65 avoid this common trap
snap sagging skin back download our free app

Back in Detroit (Fort at the Narrows)

Katherine Flannery Dering

My old house is gone. The alley where my brother
and I played has spilled out past its banks,
leaving fields of gravel, charred debris and waist-high weeds,

after months of fire, then decades of neglect.
No brick bungalows, no tiny garages or neat gardens.
Former yards and foundations merge in lakes of crabgrass

and nettle, with chunks of broken concrete, metal scraps,
and pottery shards lurking on the murky bottom.
Gone the Kercheval Live Poultry Mart.

The Chrysler assembly plant– shuttered. Even St. Rose,
where my parents were married, was torn down.
My old school's an empty brick shell.

Can this be Beniteau Street? I sit on the curb
and make out the house number, still painted there.
From above, a cascade of leaves of the weeping

birch I helped my grandfather plant, swing
in the wind. Finger-sized leaves trail around me
to the dusty ground, fall– green and silver.

H.E. Fisher

I once worked the graveyard shift at a photo printing factory and saw
other people's memories slip from machines that washed 35mm film
in chemicalized paper. My job was to take the photos the developers
spat out, check for errors, and stick the color prints into envelopes:
tireless dimensions of magic hour toasts, ring-shaped mouths and
children's firsts, chains of chained smiles— prints of lingering chroma.

We say a picture is taken.

I used to love photomats, those freestanding booths that looked like
the ones on causeways like where Sonny was shot in *The Godfather*, a
scene that takes place on Long Island, my childhood home.

My prints are in albums my children will inherit. They will go
through them and make decisions.

In the fall of my senior year in college I dreamed my mother called
me on a black rotary phone. The handset shook as it rang like in an
old Warner Bros. cartoon. I awoke to my brother's call telling me she
was dead.

Without a photograph, I'm unable to recall what my mother looked
like; there's no afterimage. Like Josef Albers' color theories, she is
wheel, light, tone absorbed and transferred.

Now and then at the factory, I would find an image spit out from the
machine in gray-scale. An error like a declaration –

I am what I see.
I am what I see.

Review of *The Diary of Saint Marion* by Gloria Monaghan

Linda Carney-Goodrich

In Gloria Monaghan's seventh book of poetry, *The Diary of Saint Marion (Found in a Laundry Basket in Hamtramck, Detroit 1971)* newly released by Lily Poetry Review Books (2025), we encounter profound imagery, deep mysticism, the natural world as witness and ever present familial stories. Memories real and imagined haunt and illuminate throughout this moving collection divided into sections; Relics, The Chalice, For Martha and Sister Juanita, Dog Poems, and I, too, Have a Chartreuse Cat.

Relics spring forth and are made new in poems on found or remembered items, some going back a century. They include an opera bag, a found diary, handwritten notes, garden tools, and black and white photographs, which leave the reader humming with a palpable sense of nostalgia, desire, and loss. With Monaghan's terrific restraint and deft imagery, we can almost feel these items in our hands. The soft feel of a small bag in "Opera Bag" leaves the narrator to wonder, "… whether I tell / the truth about beauty and what is lost." This is a musing that echoes through the book, along with the inherent contradiction of writing "truth" about items both real and imagined that were once touched, written upon, or used in everyday life of loved ones now lost. The entire collection grapples with loss and beauty found in memory.

Lovely questions emerge; what do items left behind tell us of those who went before and can there be greater truth revealed in the construction of poems, which by their nature, force both poet and reader to fill in unknowable details? What untold family stories and memories might we carry in our bodies, always at work somewhere below the surface? What unnamed relics might our own bodies hold? Monaghan liberates herself and her grandmother Marion from the fallibility of the earthly realm which is constrained by limitations of time, imperfect memory, and lived experience. She does this by rendering her grandmother a saint. The poems are told from the perspective of a supernatural-like Marion, who is able to move in, out and through time. This transcendent, almost ecstatic quality is felt throughout the book. Monaghan is in the realm of the metaphysical conjuring both disorientation and familiarity. We feel "the circles of forever" and know without question that each ancestor "has a handprint on your soul."

Monaghan delivers moments of exquisite, if disturbing, beauty. Trees appear throughout the book almost as if family or witnesses. In "I am Not Afraid of Storms," the narrator parts ways with a lover on a train and muses over how she may actually like storms. She worries the tulip tree (which has made another appearance in the book) could split and smash in a storm.

> *I hugged the tulip tree*
> *as if it could divide me, and I would be a fig again*
> *with meticulous seeds and divine divides,*
> *stickiness inherent in my veins*
> *like the callow lies of my grandfather.*

These lines have a satisfying sound quality and an almost ineffable dual meaning, perhaps pertaining to epigenetics and trauma contained within families, but also in possibility of new division and divination. The divine presence of trees in Mognhan's book approaches the mystical. Oak, willows, and tulip trees figure prominently and stand compelling as both literal figures and metaphoric. Branches, leaves, acorns remind us throughout that, "If you can grow on a tree, you can grow anywhere." In "Twinning Acorns," the would-be reader is implored to, "Mark yourself, a hero. Emerge. / Let the fine dust settle on your green leaves"... and to "find your neighborhood is a garden." We gather that trees may know more about the subjects of the poems than the writer or reader can alone. While they contain a certain melancholic knowing, the trees also offer hope, comfort, acceptance, and new possibility.

The Diary of Saint Marion touches on family stories both known and reconstructed from a trail of objects left behind, such as a garage filled with a grandmother's old garden tools and a great grandmother's gardening gloves, all still smelling of dirt. In "Garage", the grandmothers' hands come to the speaker's mind, "brown spotted" and convey a deeper meaning of how one can be in conversation, in touch with long gone family members and ancestors. "*Help me to plant,* I say to the silence".... begs the question of who might be listening. Of course, there is a God that the narrator hints at, and the ancestors themselves, but we as the readers also hear this prayer and can't help but think of our own.

There is something of the sublime at work in this collection. For example, in "Car Thief" there is a feeling of a self conscious narrator making observations in moments forever suspended in time within the container of a poem. One can sense the poet's musings over creative choices and the different truths they could render, as in "Martha's brother drove the car himself, / I put her in the back" and in the last line, "as he faced oncoming traffic, these are the things I think about." These lines could be from multiple viewpoints. Monaghan evokes in the reader a sense of replaying/rewatching a memory with an underlying self-conscious awareness. While stepping into the real or imagined memory contained in the poem, one may choose to hone in on different angles and possible choices of both the poet and the poem's subject.

More wonderful moments of a surreal quality can be found throughout, perhaps most enjoyable in Monaghan's dog poems. In "When the Dog is more Magnificent than the Man" dogs lead men from "spies, or in a cave with bats shimmering the walls." We discover that a leash is a soul connection, "shining, beating into a mere single strand / of gold barely visible." There is whimsical possibility in "Suddenly I Become the Dog" in which the narrator somehow transforms into a dog. This is on the heels of, "Sonya the Dog" through which we learn the family dog was named after a psychologist and that the narrator "decided it would be good to play the part, / and went to the Thrift store to buy a dress from the 1950s" along with " a nurse's outfit which I wore for years." These hint at confining choices for women and girls, but also of the rich possibilities for retreat and relief found within a robust and vivid imagination. "In my youth I was a star shatterer," the narrator reveals and we feel the powerful truth of these words just waiting to be remembered and realized.

In perhaps what might be the most provocative section of *The Diary of Saint Marion*, Monaghan retells a harrowing story of Sister Janina who had disappeared in 1907 and whose bones were found buried in a church basement cellar along with those of a fetus in 1918. Martha, friend to Marion, is the pregnant housekeeper of Father Edward and is believed by the narrator to be pregnant by him. In this section, again we discover that memory along with found objects, real or imagined, work to piece together a story both factual and sur-real. Martha remembers Sister Janina and is also an insomniac who scoffs at a man who attempts to build a time machine in the desert. There is Martha's failing report card in "Walk to School with Martha" and her own children bored with her recounting of Sister Janina in "Martha Remembering Sister Janina's Bones". Then there is Martha's diary, through which we consider real and surreal possibilities and impossibilities.

In the closing section of the book, there is a wonderful nod to the metaphysical poet, John Donne's "Forbidding Mourning", which suggests love and family may transcend time and distance. In "Standing in the Willow" we return to the grandmother's too small gardening gloves and tools. The narrator tells us she herself can use these "for the tougher branches too high to reach." The narra-tor considers her own hands and fingernails as grounds for buried memories and stories contained within the book. Back in the garage, the narrator is struck by a vivid scent memory, almost of ghostlike quality. "… her smell comes to me a light must, / cigarettes and something I cannot name." This feeling of longing and nostalgia is discovered, rediscovered, and reshaped throughout the book. In *The Diary of Saint Marion*, Monaghan sheds light on how family memories and secrets are revealed through both physical and mental relics handed down intergenerationally and by the meaning we each construct, whether in poems or in our own imaginations. This is a book that invites multiple readings, for it is rich in meaning, metaphor, image, and story. It hums with emotion and invitation, as in the closing poem, "Flying West" which asks the question, "Did I shed the world?" Here perhaps, a reader may ponder who is the asker of this question, the poet or a narrator or a subject? "My pain was a house," the narrator tells us, "to shut myself up in and disappear." Seeming to speak directly to the reader, the narrator requests, "If you get this, call me. / If you care to explain, put it in a song. / Shed the light of day." One can imagine Marion directing this to a lost love, a past or future relative, to the one whom the narrator says, "held my hand and sighed into my hair."

Lily Poetry Review Press, 2025, ISBN: 978-1-957755-57-1

Miriam O'Neal

A NATIVE OF PRINCE EDWARD ISLAND, longtime teacher at University of Massachusetts, Boston, where he was Director of Irish Studies from 1984-2019, and current Scholar-in-Residence at Saint Mary's College in northern Indiana, Thomas O'Grady poems are grounded in landscapes of both the Atlantic shore and on midwestern plains.

And everywhere, there are birds! Crows, herons, vultures, finches, gulls—some in congress on freshly mown wheat fields, some posturing on the roof ridge of a neighbor's house. Here, six herons rise out of their rookery and there, "newly fledged wild turkeys/ startle[ ] the sky....". It's enough to seek out one's *Peterson's Field Guide...* to trace the landscapes involved. Gulls soar and cormorants glide neck deep marking sky and shoreline. Foxes sometimes feint in setting-sun light and across this selection, from time to time, it's January again and the gray-on-gray of the river and its banks mixes with the slate and bullet tones of shore and sky while the meadows lie in wait of their colors (yellow of daffodils & goldfinch, September's burnishing, fall's scarlets) before winter lays down its gray mantle once again.

When Thomas O'Grady is not coloring the world and palpating its air with wings, he is reckoning the deep breath of music as in his sextet, "6 X 6" in which he picks up strings by Charlie Christian & Django Rhinehart and carries us along to Les Paul's 'improvised tangle of tubes and wire' past Barney Kessel's 'My Embraceable You' and Grant Green's 'Smokin' to land on Wes Montgomery's 'Naptown Blues'. List poems made of old standards, become dancefloors planked with the wood of nostalgia for a time we know wasn't really as wonderful as a thousand song titles made it out to be, but which we are still keen to imagine as bright and lovely in spite of the world that careened around that music. And when we leave all those played notes behind, they follow, the way a dove's flute is followed by a dove's silence.

O'Grady's poems are of this world, even when they call down the Greek or Roman dieties. In his triptych, "Variations on a Theme" we are reminded right from the start of "Mythos" that "We are mortal. We all must fall...." Still, the speaker can't help imagining the way two mortals deep in post-coital sleep would have looked to those dieties. In section 2, "What Saw the Gods..." we are invited to observe, along with said Gods

> *your fingers a tender cuff on my wrist*
> *your ankle in the clasping grasp of my hand —*
> *our limbs the weathered ribs, the splintered keel*
> *and mast of a half-buried shipwreck play*
> *across an uncharted desolate strand....*

And, because this is O'Grady's poem and he is a poet of place and time, he drags us back to our own era with section 3. "Boxcars," which relocates us to "these midwestern plains/ that spread in all directions like a good/ long life lived out but not done yet –". We observe the fate of boxcars shuffled onto deserted side-tracks, "in my mind always in twos...", "their doors slid wide to frame the world/ just as far as the mortal eye can see."

In the final stanza of "Boxcars" we are relocated one more time to a small café in Paris, where an aging couple sips coffee in comfortable silence. Mortality, we learn, is the realm where love may outlast myth's busybody gods....

Cows and cats and fire-fighters managing a controlled burn on an overgrown urban lot, land among O'Grady's verses as a series of guarantors that these poems are inhabited by the quotidian. His metaphors are as durable as the hermit crab, "...carrying home/ upon its back," which the speaker likens to the 'home' that "I carry [ ] in my head." And though the passage of seasons and their accompanying migrations and losses weave through these poems of place, no wound bleeds or weeps past healing. August keeps landing on the page; rich and rife with reminders, as in "Auguries"

No more playing blind
casting about
as if miscast in myth,

seeking
in the feathered beat
of birds some sign:

today, ears cupped
to the August sky, we
eyed with awe

the northern harrier's
scouring scowl across
a fresh-mown meadow.

How the domestic
turns exotic
in a time of change —

.....

What we learn from O'Grady's graceful, time-bending, light-blending, bird-, god-, and earthbound poems, is that it's always a time of change; so we might as well open ourselves wide to that exotic fact.

Arrowsmith Press, Medford, MA 2025, ISBN: 979-8-9915254-9

Review of Bone Machine Press

Rusty Barnes

BONE MACHINE PUBLISHES traditional poetry chapbooks with few frills. I like that. I also like other things that are not good for me, like reading and reviewing chapbooks. Publisher Scott Laudati's chapbook design for Bone Machine is squarely in the small press tradition: roughly trimmed at 5.5 x 8, cover stock only a bit heavier than the text, whimsically attractive covers with the same font repeated on the chaps I'm going to discuss here.

Starting with William Taylor Jr.'s *A Music Even of This*, I find – does it matter I've known and enjoyed his poetry for some time? – again a number of poems that remind me of past masters, all credit to him for knowing his forebears. Taylor sits cheek by jowl with the best of his contemporaries. In the poem Down at Turk and Taylor, the writer takes a second-person persona sitting – boom-hah! – in the Tenderloin, seeing life and death quite literally. It's a bit abstract in the suggestion, sure, but readers can fill in what's necessary pretty easily. Taylor is best when his images are concrete.

> *You can stop for a drink*
> *in some little place*
>
> *with hip hop on the jukebox*
> *and pretty girls playing pool*
>
> *where you try and get a few lines down*
> *before they're gone.*

No plastic language, no reaching for something beyond this poem at this moment. It's you, me, and everyone else in the poetic 'hood seeing anew what Taylor has chosen to show us, to "trick another moment from the world/that has already forgotten your name."

Which is not to say that it doesn t reach beyond but rather that it s
not ostentatious in the process.

❧

Victor Clevenger is another stalwart of the underground scene,
with at least eleven books to his name, though as prolific as he is I
wouldn't be surprised if it's actually more. His poetry, haibun, in this
case, come from the Midwest. There's a hard-bitten flair as well as
moments of tenderness and insight and grace. I've not read a lot of
haibun, but these seem to fit as my quick Google reveals, a typical
prose poem – 150 words or fewer – followed by a haiku that reflects or
amplifies or otherwise complicates the poem's subject(s).

In Living Color

shortly after kissing underneath a fireball sunset that
brightly burned in the distant sky   she stood there
singing etta james while showering   a thick layer
of soap suds on the washrag she drug across her
chest before moving down to her stomach
her hips   her ass

the beauty of
closing your eyes & still
seeing everything

What I like is the plain-spoken first two lines, preparatory to
the haiku-end. They don'ot oversell the image nor make it reach
too far: So image followed by elevated prose. Images of the woman
showering, yes, felt-life detail, yes, then, the haiku, linking to the
speaker's memory and thus the reader's. Good stuff. I'll be watching
for more from Bone Machine.

A Music Even of This – William Taylor Jr.
The Aching Season – Victor Clevenger

Rusty Barnes

M.P. CARVER'S CHAPBOOK *Hard Up*, published by the always-worth-the-time Lily Poetry Review Books, sneaks up on the reader in the most innocent of ways. She immediately lets us know what the reader can expect from her poems. She quotes every food-service supervisor's pissy mantra – "if you have time to lean, you have time to clean." –
as the title of the second poem. The rawest of poets might find here an invitation to slag on salaried managers, but Carver refuses the easy comparisons.

> *I was*
> *starting out*
> *at fourteen*
>
> *too young*
> *to touch*
> *anything but*
>
> *the register.*
> *McDonald's*
> *said they*
>
> *recorded us*
> *for safety*
> *but really*
>
> *it was to*
> *catch workers*
> *stealing.*

Issues of class are never far away in this world. Carver has mastered the deceptively charged, deftly made, short lyric as well as the narrative. In the poem "Capitalism," the narrator renders the felt-life detail so well it compels the reader to ponder the witty and self-reflection as in the "but after we could sit side by side / and watch even the sun depreciate."

Another stellar poem – my favorite – comes near the end of the chapbook. "Rich People Spend Their Money" imagines a speaker uncomfortable in the homes of the rich and their "bric a bracs," which they feel are fit only to be dented, and damaged, so the rich are "instead of focusing on all that money."

Hard Up isn't just a book of poems, it's a personal history of individual resilience and humor in the face of ineffective work ethic. It disfavors the advantage the well-off take for granted when we know already that, as the saying goes, there is there is no ethical consumption under capitalism. I'm no Marxist, but I know something of the way the world works, and so does M.P. Carver.

Lily Poetry Review Press, 2025, ISBN: 978-1-957755-57-1

Biographies

Author

L. Acadia is a lit professor at NTU and Taiwan Literature Base Writer-in-Residence with poetry in *New Orleans Review, Strange Horizons, trampset,* and elsewhere. Lilith lives with her wife and hound in the 'literature mountain' district of Taipei.
Connect at www.acadiaink.com or social media: @acadialogue

Rusty Barnes lives in Revere MA with his family. He's published 16 books in the small press, most recently a chapbook of poems called *DEAR So & So* and a collection of stories called *HALF CRIME.*

Jonathan Blunk's authorized biography, *James Wright: A Life in Poetry* (Farrar, Straus and Giroux, 2017), earned praise from The *New York Times Book Review*, where it was an Editors' Choice. *The Georgia Review* has published his essays and reviews, with upcoming new work. Blunk's poems have appeared in *FIELD* and other journals, including new poems in *The Ekphrastic Review.*

Annie Bolger is a poet living in Boston, Massachusetts. She is a winner of the Lois Morrell poetry contest, and her work is published or forthcoming in *tsuri-dōrō, r.kv.ry quarterly,* and *Small Craft,* among others. She holds a B.A. from Swarthmore College.
Find her at annieb.ink.

Sarah Carleton writes poetry, edits fiction, plays the banjo, and knits obsessively in Tampa, Florida. Her poems have appeared in numerous publications, including *ONE ART, Valparaiso, SWWIM, As It Ought to Be,* and *Rattle.* Sarah's first collection, *Notes from the Girl Cave,* was published in 2020 by Kelsay Books.

Linda Carney-Goodrich is a writer and teacher from Boston. Her first book of poetry, *Dot Girl* (Nixes Mate Books, 2024) was a finalist for the New England Poetry Club's Sheila Margaret Motton Prize. Her poems have been displayed at Boston City Hall and have appeared in *Lily Poetry Review, The MacGuffin, Literary Mama, Muddy River, Anti-Heroin Chic,* and *Gyroscope*

Review, among others. Linda is the Poetry Coordinator for the Menino Art Center in Hyde Park and owner of Home Scholars of Boston.

Alex Carrigan (he/him) is the author of *Now Let's Get Brunch* (Querencia Press, 2023) and *May All Our Pain Be Champagne* (Alien Buddha Press, 2022).

Susan Michele Coronel's first full-length collection, *In the Needle, A Woman*, won the 2024 Donna Wolf Palacio Poetry Prize, and is forthcoming from Finishing Line Press. A two-time Pushcart nominee, she has had poems published in numerous journals including *MOM Egg Review, Spillway 29, Redivider*, and *One Art*.

Melanie DuBose lives under camphor trees filled with parrots in Los Angeles (Highland Park). Her prose and poetry have been published in many journals including the *Ekphrastic Review, Kelp/the Wave, The Los Angeles Press*, and *New Verse News*. She recently finished writing her first novel, *People Who Love You*.

Roseanne English holds an MFA from NYU and is working on her first collection. She lives in the Hudson Valley.

H.E. Fisher is the author of the collection *Sterile Field* (Free Lines Press, 2022) and the chapbook *Jane Almost Always Smiles* (Moonstone Arts Center Press, 2022). H.E. was awarded City College of New York's 2019 Stark Poetry Prize and has received nominations for Best of the Net and The Pushcart Prize.

Katherine Flannery Dering has published a memoir, *Shot in the Head, a Sister's Memoir a Brother's Struggle* (Bridgeross), a mixed genre book of prose, poetry, photos, and emails. Her first chapbook, *Aftermath*, was published by Finishing Line Press. Some of her poetry and essays have appeared recently in *Inkwell Magazine, River Six Hens, Tilde, Cordella, Can We Have Our Ball Back?, Adanna, Panoplyzine, Book of Matches*, and *Gossamer*.

Jennifer Franklin is the author of three poetry collections, including *If Some God Shakes Your House* (Four Way), finalist for the Paterson Prize and Julie Suk Award. Her work has been commissioned by The Metropolitan Museum, and published in *American Poetry Review, The Paris Review*, "poem-a-day" on poets.org, and Poetry Society of America's "Poetry in Motion." She won a Pushcart Prize, a NYFA grant, and a CRCF Award. Her new manuscript, *A Fire In Her Brain* is a series of epistolary poems to Virginia Woolf, Lucia Joyce, and Sylvia Plath. She is the cofounder of "Words Like Blades" reading series. She teaches in Manhattanville's MFA program as well as Poets House, The Frost Place, 24Pearl Street & her own manuscript revision workshops.

Richard Hoffman's nine books include the Massachusetts Book Award winning *Noon until Night*, and the recent *People Once Real*. He is Emeritus Writer-in-Residence at Emerson College and nonfiction editor of *Solstice: A Magazine of Diverse Voices*.

Ann Hostetler is the author of two collections of poetry, *Safehold* (2018) and *Empty Room with Light* (2002), and the editor of *A Cappella: Mennonite Voices in Poetry* (Iowa 2003). Her poems have appeared in *The American Scholar, Poet Lore, Valparaiso Poetry Review* and many other journals and anthologies. The poem in this issue are from her new manuscript, *Penelope Among the Roosters*. She is professor of English Emerita at Goshen College in Goshen, IN where she taught literature and creative writing for 22 years. She edits the *Journal of Mennonite Writing* at www.mennonitewriting.org.

Lauren Leja is the author of two books of short fiction, *Air & other stories*, and *Rotor* both by Nixes Mate Books. Her book of photography, *Invisible Commute* cataloged her daily commute.

Jennifer Markell's first poetry collection, *Samsara*, (Turning Point, 2014) was named a "Must Read" by the Massachusetts Book Awards. The Main Street Rag published *Singing at High Altitude* in 2021. Her poems have appeared in *The Bitter Oleander, Consequence, Cutthroat Diode, RHINO, Storm Cellar*, and others.

Kevin McLellan is the author of: *Sky. Pond. Mouth.* (winner of the 2024 Granite State Poetry Prize selected by Alexandria Peary and a finalist for the Thom Gunn Award in Poetry); *in other words you/* (winner of the 2022 Hilary Tham Capital Collection selected by Timothy Liu); *Ornitheology; Tributary; Round Trip* and the book objects, *Hemispheres* and *[box]* which reside in several special collections including the Blue Star Collection at Harvard University.

David P. Miller's *Bend in the Stair* was published by Lily Poetry Review Books in 2021. *Sprawled Asleep* was published by Nixes Mate Books in 2019. His poems have appeared in journals including *Meat for Tea, Reed Magazine, About Place Journal, Solstice, Salamander, Tar River Poetry*, and *Vincent Brothers Review*.

Gloria Mindock is editor of Červená Barva Press, an award-winning author of six poetry collections, two book translations into Romanian and Serbian, and three chapbooks. Her poems have been widely published and translated into twelve languages. Her recent book, *Grief Touched the Sky at Night*, was published by Glass Lyre Press. Gloria was the Poet Laureate in Somerville, MA in 2017 & 2018.

Miriam O'Neal has 3 books of poems in print. Her poetry and reviews have appeared in *Galway Review, Los Angeles Review of Books, North Dakota Quarterly*, and elsewhere. Her most recent collection, *The Half-Said Things*, was published by Nixes Mate Books in 2022.

Mary Pinard is the author of two books of poetry: *Portal* and *Ghost Heart*. Her poems have also appeared in a range of literary journals and anthologies, most recently *Ecotone and Moving Images: Poetry Inspired by Cinema*. She teaches literature and poetry in the Arts & Humanities Division at Babson College.

Kyle Potvin's full-length poetry collection is *Loosen*. Her chapbook, *Sound Travels on Water*, won the Jean Pedrick Chapbook Award, and Kyle won The Patricia Eschen Prize for Poetry 2024– Sonnet Award. Kyle's poems have appeared in *Bellevue Literary Review, Tar River Poetry, Verse Daily* and *The New York Times*.

Christy Prahl's collections include *We Are Reckless* (Cornerstone Press, 2023), *With Her Hair on Fire* (Roadside Press, forthcoming fall 2025), and *Catalog of Labors* (Unsolicited Press, forthcoming 2026). A Best of the Net and Pushcart Prize nominee, her work has been featured in *Poetry Daily* and elsewhere. More at christyprahl.wixsite.com/christy-prahl.

Brad Rose is the author of six collections of poetry and flash fiction: *WordInEdgeWise, Lucky Animals, No. Wait. I Can Explain, Pink X-Ray, de/tonations*, and *Momentary Turbulence*. His poetry collection, *I Wouldn't Say*

That, Exactly, is forthcoming. Brad's poetry and fiction have appeared in, *The American Journal of Poetry, The Los Angeles Times, Baltimore Review, New York Quarterly, Lunch Ticket, Puerto del Sol, Clockhouse, Folio, Best Microfiction* (2019), *Action Spectacle, Right Hand Pointing*, and other journals and anthologies. His website is www.bradrosepoetry.com
Selected audio readings: bradrosepoetry.com/audio-readings/

William Ross is a Canadian writer and visual artist living in Toronto. His poems have appeared in *Rattle, The New Quarterly, Humana Obscura, Bicoastal Review, Underscore Magazine, Amethyst Review, Bindweed Magazine Anthology, The Hooghly Review, Heavy Feather Review, Anti-Heroin Chic*, and others.

Lisa Schapiro Flynn has published poems in journals including *Radar Poetry, Bluestem, The Crab Creek Review, The Tishman Review*, and others. She received an Honorable Mention for the 2018 Crab Creek Review Poetry Prize judged by Maggie Smith. Lisa has an MFA in poetry from Emerson College. She lives in New York with her family.

Kurt Schmidt's stories have appeared in the *Boston Globe, Discretionary Love, Storyhouse, The Examined Life Journal, Eclectica Magazine*, and others. He is also the author of the novel *Annapolis Misfit* (Crown Publishers). He is currently finishing a 30-year memoir about parenting a risk-taker. www. kurtgschmidt.com

Alex Stolis lives in Minneapolis; he has had poems published in numerous journals. Two full length collections *Pop. 1280*, and *John Berryman Died Here* were released by Cyberwit. His work has previously appeared or is forthcoming in *Piker's Press, Jasper's Folly Poetry Journal, Beatnik Cowboy, One Art Poetry, Black Moon Magazine*, and *Star 82 Review*. His chapbook, *Postcards from the Knife-Thrower's Wife*, was released by Louisiana Literature Press in 2024, *RIP Winston Smith* from Alien Buddha Press 2024, and *The Hum of Geometry; The Music of Spheres*, 2024 by Bottlecap Press.

Kerry Trautman lives in Ohio, USA. Her work has appeared previously in *Nixes Mate*, as well as numerous other journals and anthologies. Her books are *Things That Come in Boxes; To Have Hoped; Artifacts; To be Nonchalantly Alive; Marilyn: Self-Portrait, Oil on Canvas; Unknowable Things;* and *Irregulars.*

Alice G. Waldert is an emerging poet. Her work has appeared in literary
journals across the United States, Canada, and the United Kingdom. She
is working on a collection of poems about her experiences as a foster child.
She holds an M.A. in Canadian Studies and an MFA in writing.

Ann E. Wallace is Poet Laureate Emeritus of Jersey City, NJ and host of
"The WildStory: A Podcast of Poetry and Plants." She is the author of two
poetry collections: *Days of Grace* and *Silence: A Chronicle of COVID's Long
Haul* (Kelsay Books, 2024) and *Counting by Sevens* (Main Street Rag, 2019).
You can follow her online at AnnWallacePhD.com and on Instagram @
annwallace409.

William Webb lives in Berkeley, California. He is a Faculty Associate
and is on the Advisory Board of the Institute of Writing and Thinking
at Bard College where he teaches educators how to create and sustain a
writing-based classroom. He is a writer, a cook, a teacher, a swimmer and
collector of neighborhood cast-offs. He and his husband and their dog
Turnip can often be found in the hills walking or on the couch napping.
He has published in *Field Notes, La Voz, the NAIS Magazine,* and *Anthem.*

Colophon

The text is set in Maiola, a contemporary typeface inspired by early Czech type design. The titles are set in Tablet Gothic, a grotesque sans-serif grounded in 19th century British typography. Both fonts were designed by Veronika Burian, a type designer and co-founder of the independent type foundry TypeTogether. She is also involved with Alphabettes.org, a showcase of work and research on lettering, typography, and type design by women.

SUBSCRIBE TO NIXES MATE REVIEW.

Get 2 issues per year for $25.
Go to nixesmate.pub/subscribe

BECOME A PATRON OF NIXES MATE.

For $50 receive two issues of *Nixes Mate Review*, plus our latest book, and a special literary treat.

For $100 receive two issues of *Nixes Mate Review*, plus our latest three books, and a special literary treat.

For $250 receive two issues of *Nixes Mate Review*, plus our latest three books, and all the available limited edition broadsides.

For $500 receive two issues of *Nixes Mate Review*, plus all the books in our catalog.

For $1000 receive all current and future issues of *Nixes Mate Review*, plus all the books in our catalog, all the available limited edition broadsides and chapbooks, various special literary treats, and all our future books.

42° 19' 47.9" N · 70° 56' 43.9" W

Nixes Mate is a navigational hazard in Boston Harbor used during the colonial period to gibbet and hang pirates and mutineers.

Nixes Mate Books features small-batch artisanal literature, created by writers who use all 26 letters of the alphabet and then some, honing their craft the time-honored way: one line at a time.

nixesmate.pub